PUFFIN BO[...]

THE PUFFIN BOOK OF ROYAL LONDON

Which British queen thought the drains ponged at Windsor Castle? Which king walked across St James's Park to his execution? Which one was carried away from a party with his clothes covered in jelly and cream, and which one died on the loo?

Answers to questions you would never even have thought of asking, and many more riveting royal facts are in *The Puffin Book of Royal London*. You can find out about the royal palaces of London, from the Tower of London to Windsor Castle, from Greenwich Palace to Hampton Court. You probably know that the Tower of London was a prison, but did you know it was also a zoo, a royal home and an armoury? Did you know that part of Westminster Palace used to be the Royal Treasury and that Whitehall began life as York Place, the London home of the Archbishops of York? And almost every palace in London had a large hunting-park nearby so that the monarchs and their visitors could enjoy a spot of hunting. And, of course, every royal palace of London was near the River Thames so that the kings and queens could avoid the crush on the streets!

Nowadays, everyone can enjoy these palaces and parks and learn a little more about our kings and queens, whether it's through a visit to London or simply sitting in an armchair and reading this book!

Scoular Anderson was born in Dunoon in Argyllshire and educated at Keil School. He studied graphic design at Glasgow School of Art, spent a few years as artist in residence at London University, then taught art in secondary schools for about ten years. He is now a full-time illustrator and author. His first book for Puffin was *A Plunder of Pirates*.

Also by Scoular Anderson

A PLUNDER OF PIRATES

The Puffin Book of
Royal London

Scoular Anderson

PUFFIN BOOKS

For P.D.

PUFFIN BOOKS

Published by the Penguin Group
Penguin Books Ltd, 27 Wrights Lane, London W8 5TZ, England
Viking Penguin, a division of Penguin Books USA Inc.
375 Hudson Street, New York, New York 10014, USA
Penguin Books Australia Ltd, Ringwood, Victoria, Australia
Penguin Books Canada Ltd, 2801 John Street, Markham, Ontario, Canada L3R 1B4
Penguin Books (NZ) Ltd, 182–190 Wairau Road, Auckland 10, New Zealand

Penguin Books Ltd, Registered Offices: Harmondsworth, Middlesex, England

First published 1991
1 3 5 7 9 10 8 6 4 2

Text and illustrations copyright © Scoular Anderson, 1991
All rights reserved

The moral right of the author/illustrator has been asserted

Printed in England by Clays Ltd, St Ives plc
Filmset in Monophoto Bembo

Except in the United States of America,
this book is sold subject to the condition
that it shall not, by way of trade or otherwise,
be lent, re-sold, hired out, or otherwise circulated
without the publisher's prior consent in any form of
binding or cover other than that in which it is
published and without a similar condition
including this condition being imposed
on the subsequent purchaser

Contents

To Begin With . . . — 1

Map of London
Showing Situations of Palaces — 4

Westminster Palace
Floods and Fishy Business — 5

It's Quicker by Boat
Royal River Transport — 11

The Tower
Beefeaters and Beheadings — 14

Richmond Palace
Gallantry on the Green — 30

Windsor Castle
Garters and Gruesome Drains — 32

A Spot of Sport
The Royal Parks — 38

Greenwich Palace
Ships and Puddles — 46

Flutes and Fireworks
Music at Court — 54

Whitehall Palace
Damp and Draughty 58

Cheers and Chivalry
The Royal Tilt-yards 64

Hampton Court Palace
Marvels and Mazes 68

All Glass and Gilt
The Royal Coaches 74

Kensington Palace
Highwaymen and Wild Boys 78

Towser and the Lions
Some Royal Beasts 83

St James's Palace
Wear the Right Wig 86

Salt and Sweetmeats
Royal Meals 90

Buckingham Palace
No Silkworms or Sinks 92

Handy List of Monarchs 96

Ghosts 100

Index 101

To Begin With...

The word palace comes from the name of one of the hills in the ancient city of Rome – the Palatine Hill. On this hill stood the magnificent house of the Roman Emperors – the Caesars – which is said to have covered the entire hill.

Nowadays the word palace can mean any grand building, but this book is about a special group of palaces – the royal palaces of London – where the kings and queens of Britain lived and where the present Queen lives today.

Once, our monarchs lived in castles – for safety reasons! When the country became more secure, they moved out into more spacious homes. These palaces grew grander as the centuries passed. It was not because the monarchs were spendthrift (though some undoubtedly were!). In order to keep the country peaceful, it was necessary for the monarchs to show their power, importance and wealth to their people and to rulers of other countries. How better to do this than in a magnificent palace filled with tapestries, paintings, music and mouthwatering banquets!

Most of our monarchs lived in several palaces, constantly moving from one to another, depending on the seasons or the business of State.

They all had their favourites – and the ones they hated! For instance, Greenwich was Henry VIII's favourite palace, while Queen Mary I and Queen Anne preferred St James's.

George III said he didn't like Hampton Court because of the memory of his grandfather hitting him on the ears when he was a boy.

TO BEGIN WITH...

William III and his wife Mary hated Whitehall – it was bad for William's asthma and Mary said...

All I can see is water and wall.

wheeze wheeze

The drains at Windsor were faulty. They are said to have caused the death of Prince Albert, Queen Victoria's husband.

Maybe Buckingham Palace once had the same problem, because Edward VIII said...

There's always a musty smell in here

Map of London
Showing Situations of Palaces

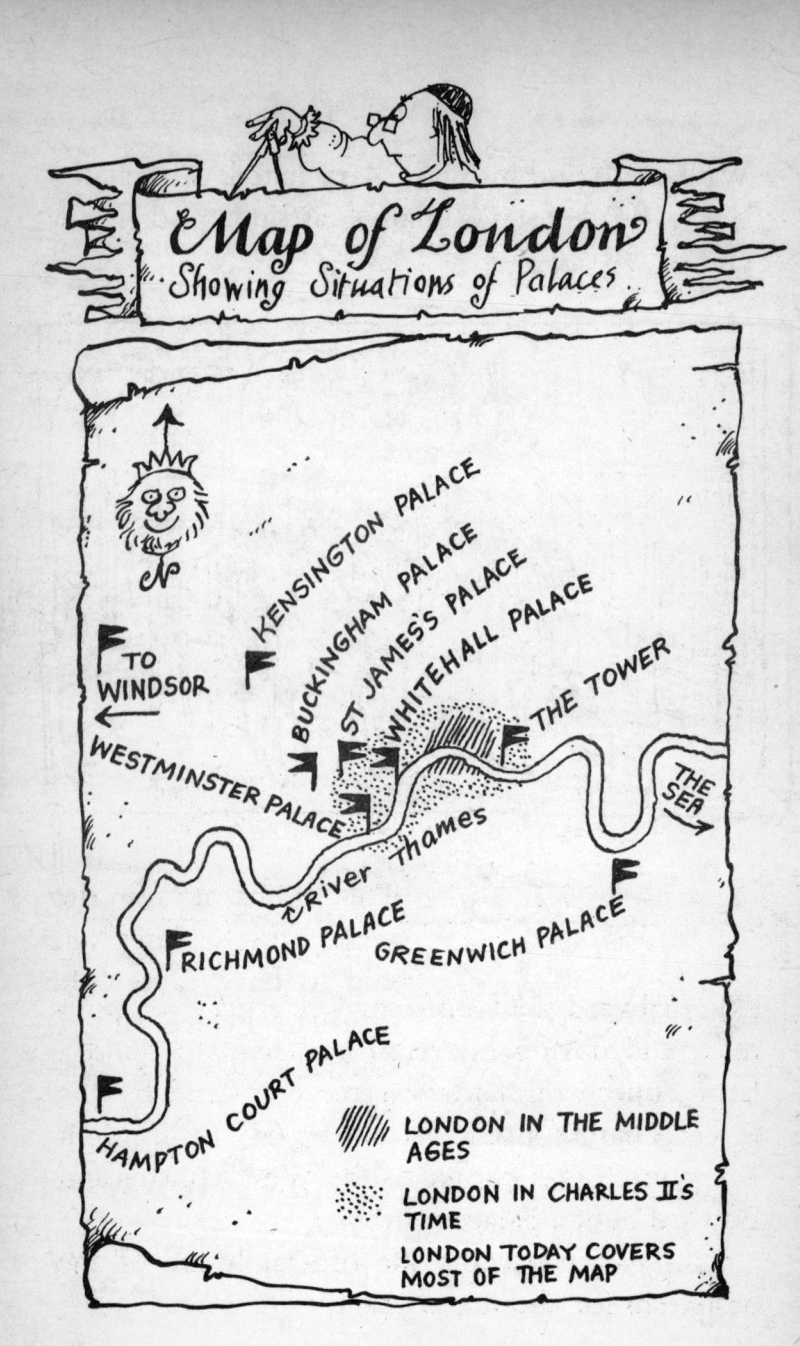

- KENSINGTON PALACE
- BUCKINGHAM PALACE
- ST JAMES'S PALACE
- WHITEHALL PALACE
- THE TOWER
- WESTMINSTER PALACE
- RICHMOND PALACE
- GREENWICH PALACE
- HAMPTON COURT PALACE

← TO WINDSOR

River Thames → THE SEA

///// LONDON IN THE MIDDLE AGES

····· LONDON IN CHARLES II's TIME

LONDON TODAY COVERS MOST OF THE MAP

Westminster Palace
Floods and Fishy Business

Richard II's Hall at Westminster

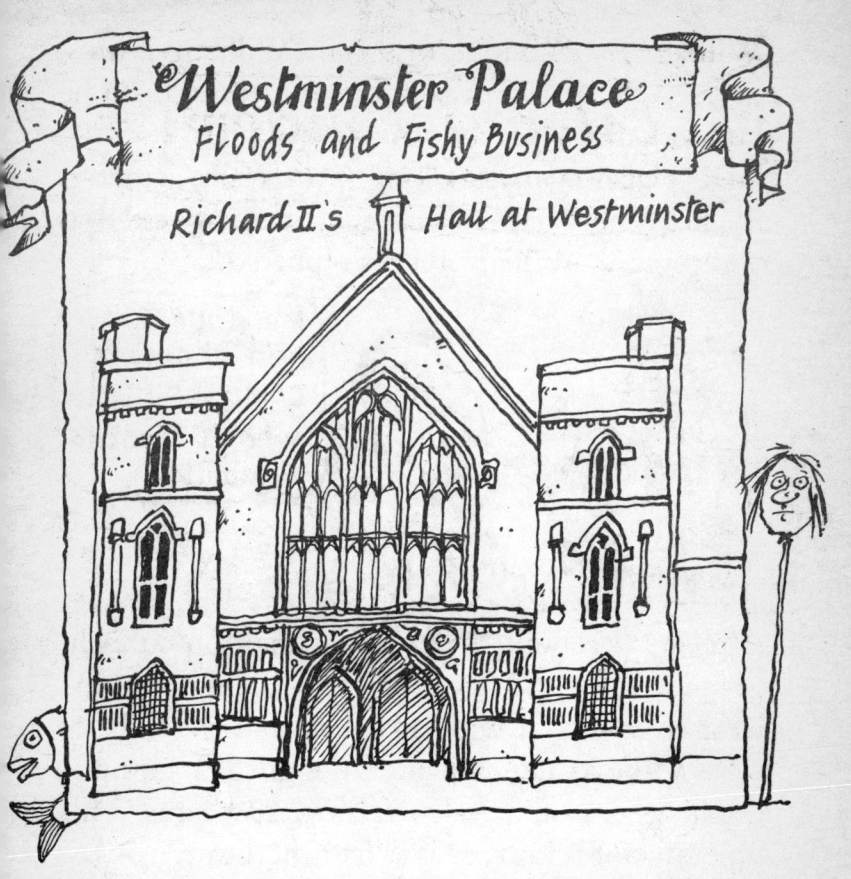

King Edward the Confessor was a very religious man, and during his reign he began to build a large church on a marshy piece of land by the River Thames, not far from the city of London. The church was known as the West Minster and Edward built a palace nearby.

This palace became the official home of the monarchs for about 400 years.

THE PUFFIN BOOK OF ROYAL LONDON

William the Conqueror's son, William Rufus, decided the palace was not grand enough, so he built a hall for gatherings and banquets. It was a huge place 72 metres long with walls 2 metres thick. When one of his courtiers suggested it was too big, William Rufus replied ...

It's a mere bed-chamber compared to what I wanted to build.

Richard II rebuilt Westminster Hall on an even grander scale. So that the roof could support itself over such a wide span without the help of pillars, the chief carpenter designed a complicated system of wooden arches and beams. This type of roof is known as a 'hammerbeam' roof.

When it was finished, Richard celebrated with a lavish banquet.

Hammerbeam Roof

WESTMINSTER PALACE

Thereafter, the hall had a colourful history.

During coronation banquets, it was traditional for the king's champion to ride into the hall on horseback and challenge any traitor to a fight.

It was quite common for floods to wash mud and fish into the hall from the nearby River Thames. One year, men even rowed boats into the hall.

It was used for a while as a court of law and in the seventeenth century as a shopping precinct where you could buy books, clothes, hats and toys.

For a while, Oliver Cromwell's head, along with the heads of two of his companions, sat on stakes at one end of the hall.

In 1303, a merchant called Richard de Podlicote carried out a daring raid – he broke into the Royal Treasury at Westminster with the help of twelve monks from the nearby Abbey. The royal treasure, including the King's crown, was kept in the Chapel of the Pyx, which had immensely thick walls and double oak doors with seven locks.

Podlicote escaped with a fortune (though he left the crown) but he was soon caught, sentenced and killed. It is said that his skin was nailed to the treasury door.

A more secure treasury was built. It was called the Jewel Tower and looked like a miniature castle, complete with moat. The keeper, William Ussheborne, put fish into the moat, but came to an unfortunate end when he ate one for dinner and choked.

The Jewel Tower today

All that remains of the Palace of Westminster today is the Jewel Tower and the Great Hall (as built by Richard II). The Hall is part of the Houses of Parliament, which are still sometimes called (confusingly) the Palace of Westminster.

The Houses of Parliament

It's Quicker by Boat
Royal River Transport

Before the invention of cars, trains and buses, the River Thames was used much more as a means of transport than it is today. The streets and lanes of old London were narrow and twisting, so it was often quicker to travel the length of the city by boat.

Most of the royal palaces were built by the river so that royalty could travel from one palace to another in a royal barge and avoid the crush!

Royal barges were very ornate. When Anne Boleyn (one of Henry VIII's wives) sailed to her coronation, she was accompanied by hundreds of other boats. Some had bells tied to their rigging. One barge carried a giant dragon of painted cloth which spouted fire.

At the wedding procession of Charles II and Catherine of Braganza, the river was filled with barges decorated with flags, pavilions and fanciful beasts.

Prince Frederick's Barge

IT'S QUICKER BY BOAT

At a regatta at Woolwich in 1749, the oarsmen were dressed in Chinese costume.

Prince Frederick's barge was built in 1731. The Prince (son of George II) was so keen to try it out that on the very day it was put in the water, he sailed to Somerset House to inspect the cleaning of the royal paintings. The barge was used by monarchs until Prince Albert made the last voyage in 1849.

The Tower
Beefeaters and Beheadings

The Tower is one of London's most spectacular buildings. It's also a place with a long and colourful history of pageants and banquets, tortures, beheadings, ghosts and many other strange happenings.

Although Westminster Palace was the monarch's official residence, the Tower was a palace too, especially in times of danger. It was also an arsenal (for keeping weapons), the Royal Mint (for making coins), a barracks (for housing soldiers) and a prison (for unfortunate enemies). For a time it was even a zoo.

The building of the Tower began in William the Conqueror's reign. Gundulf, Bishop of Rochester, was put in charge because he was a man 'skilful at building in stone'.

A great fortress was built first, then walls were constructed around it. The fortress is the tall building in the middle of the courtyard. It is known as the White Tower because it was once whitewashed. Nowadays the whole collection of fortifications is known as the Tower.

For centuries after William the Conqueror's reign, the Tower was enlarged and improved.

The monarch's apartments were originally in the White Tower, but eventually other towers and buildings around the courtyard were used as royal residences. It was a tradition that the new monarch lived in the Tower before moving through the city in a grand procession for his or her coronation. Charles II was the last monarch to live in the Tower, and the coronation processions were abandoned after he died.

The White Tower now houses the Royal Armouries Museum, but there are many other named towers.

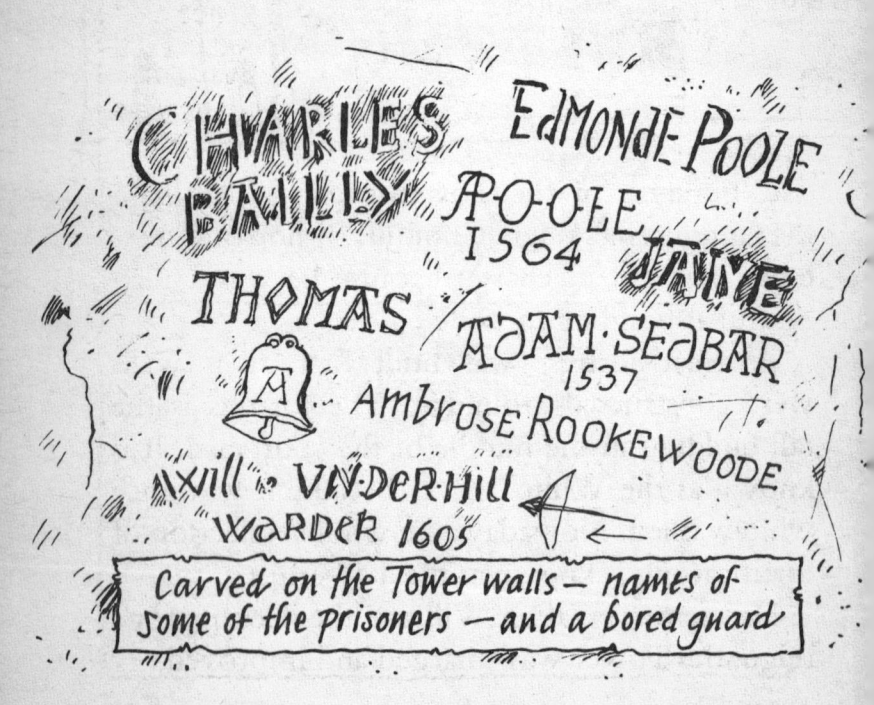

CHARLES BAILLY
EDMONDE POOLE
POOLE 1564
JANE
THOMAS
ADAM SEABAR 1537
Ambrose Rookewoode
will VNDERHILL
WARDER 1605

Carved on the Tower walls — names of some of the prisoners — and a bored guard

THE TOWER

Many of the other towers were used as prisons and on their walls you can see graffiti carved by bored prisoners. The Beauchamp Tower was a prison for many noblemen and women.

The Bloody Tower houses the machinery to lift the portcullis from the gateway below. The tower was given its sinister name because of several murders that took place in it.

It was in the Bowyer Tower in 1478 that the Duke of Clarence is said to have drowned in a butt of Malmsey wine.

THE TOWERS
DEVEREUX..
FLINT..
BOWYER..
BRICK..
MARTIN..
BROAD ARROW..
SALT..
LANTHORN..
DEVLIN..
CRADLE..
WELL..
WAKEFIELD..
ST THOMAS'S..
BLOODY..
BELL..
BYWARD..
BEAUCHAMP..
MIDDLE..
WARDROBE..
CONSTABLE..

THE PUFFIN BOOK OF ROYAL LONDON

The traditional guardians of the Tower are often called 'Beefeaters', but their correct name is 'Yeoman Warders'. Their duties were guarding the prisoners and the gates, but nowadays they look after security and visitors to the Tower.

On ceremonial occasions, the Yeoman Warders carry partisans (a type of spear) and the Chief Yeoman Warder carries a mace. The Yeoman Gaoler carries an axe. It used to be his job to accompany prisoners to and from their trial. The blade of the axe was carried pointing away from the prisoner, but if he was found guilty the blade was then turned towards him (execution would probably follow!).

THE TOWER

There have always been ravens in the Tower. They probably originally came to feed on the scraps thrown out by the inhabitants. Legend has it that if the ravens leave the Tower, then the Tower and the kingdom will fall.

In Charles II's time, the Astronomer Royal complained that the ravens were interfering with his observations of the planets. (The astronomer was moved, rather than the ravens.) Today, one of the Yeoman Warders, called the Raven Master, looks after the ravens. There are six official ravens. They have a cage in the Wakefield Tower, and even their own cemetery in the empty moat.

Just recently a baby raven was born at the Tower. It was the first to have been hatched since the reign of Charles II, over 300 years ago. This was quite an event, as ravens normally only breed in quiet places!

Prisoners and Punishments

All sorts of people became prisoners in the Tower, from kings and queens to common thieves. Conditions were not always bad. Wealthier prisoners were allowed good food and certain luxuries – books, writing materials, comfy beds, etc. There were places which were occasionally used for dangerous prisoners. They were known as Little Ease and the Dungeon Among the Rats – no more than holes in the ground where a prisoner could hardly move.

Prisoners were usually brought to the Tower by boat and entered through the water-gate, just below the Bloody Tower. The gate is now known as the Traitor's Gate. Arrival by river avoided escape attempts or noisy demonstrations from townsfolk.

THE TOWER

There were certainly instruments of torture in the Tower, but it's difficult to know exactly how many prisoners were actually tortured. Torture was used to make prisoners confess their crimes or give the names of accomplices. Often the very sight of torture instruments made prisoners confess.

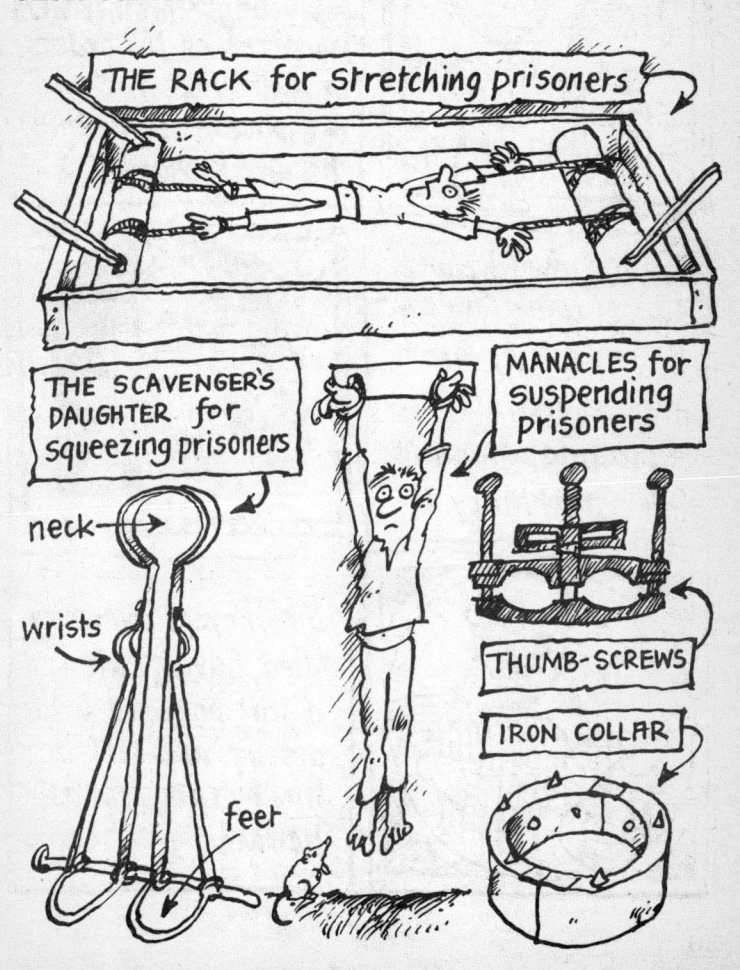

THE RACK for stretching prisoners

THE SCAVENGER'S DAUGHTER for squeezing prisoners
- neck
- wrists
- feet

MANACLES for suspending prisoners

THUMB-SCREWS

IRON COLLAR

THE PUFFIN BOOK OF ROYAL LONDON

Prisoners in the Tower – some of those detained

The Princes in the Tower: Edward V (aged 12) and his younger brother were murdered on the orders of their Uncle, Richard of Gloucester (who then became Richard III).

For a time Elizabeth Tudor (later Queen Elizabeth I) was imprisoned, accused of plotting against her half sister, Mary I.

Sir Thomas Overbury died, having eaten a tart poisoned with arsenic and sent to him by Lady Frances Howard.

THE TOWER

The first prisoner in the Tower, Ranulf Flambard, Bishop of Durham, escaped down a rope smuggled to him in a flagon of wine.

Lord Nithsdale escaped dressed as a woman.

The Duchess of Somerset's daily menu in the Tower included mutton, roast veal, roast capon, rabbits, potages, sliced beef, larks, beer, wine, butter, vinegar, mustard, onions, salads, also napkins, tablecloths, good plates, glasses, etc., etc., etc., etc.

Guy Fawkes tried to blow up the Houses of Parliament. He was tortured before being executed.

23

Executions

Prisoners accused of treason were executed. For instance, it was treason to plot to kill members of the royal family, or even speak ill of them. Some monarchs used the treason laws to get rid of people they didn't like.

Ordinary people were hanged for their crimes, but those of noble rank were beheaded. Beheadings took place on Tower Hill, just outside the walls of the Tower. The townsfolk came eagerly to watch these events. Sometimes viewing-platforms were set up – sometimes they collapsed under the weight of the spectators.

The site of the BLOCK on Tower Green

THE TOWER

Noblewomen and prisoners who were popular with Londoners were executed within the walls of the Tower, on Tower Green (perhaps to avoid an embarrassing riot).

Henry VIII's second wife (Anne Boleyn) and his fifth (Catherine Howard) were both executed on Tower Green, accused of adultery.

Rather than die by the axe, Anne Boleyn asked to be beheaded with a sword, so a skilful executioner was sent from France.

The Crown Jewels

During Oliver Cromwell's government, the regalia (the monarch's crown, orb, sceptre and other jewels) were destroyed. A new set was made for the coronation of Charles II and the Martin Tower was chosen to keep it in.

A man called Talbot Edwards was appointed keeper, but as he earned no money from this, he was allowed to show the regalia to visitors for a small fee.

THE TOWER

One day, Captain Blood arrived to see the jewels. He was disguised as a clergyman and accompanied by his wife. Mrs Blood pretended to be ill, so Edwards and his wife took her into their house. Some time later, Blood sent Mrs Edwards a gift for her kindness, and so when he returned one day with three companions, Edwards treated him as a friend and invited them to view the jewels.

Once inside the Martin Tower, the keeper was overpowered. Blood took the crown and hid it under his cloak. Another man dropped the orb into his breeches. A third tried to file the sceptre in half. They didn't get far before being captured, and the regalia were safely recovered (though a bit bashed). Mysteriously enough, rather than imprisoning Blood, the King pardoned him and even gave him a pension!

After the raid, the regalia were stored more safely. For a while, the treasures were kept behind an iron grille – though it was still possible to put your hand through the grille and touch the jewels.

In 1841 they were saved just in time when a fire broke out in the nearby armoury. No one could find the Lord Chamberlain who kept the keys, so the grille had to be axed down.

Today you can see the crown jewels in the modern – and secure – Jewel House.

THE TOWER

When the Tower is locked up for the night, the ancient 'Ceremony of the Keys' takes place.

The Chief Yeoman Warder and his escort lock the outer gates then, as they arrive at the gate of the Bloody Tower, they meet the main Tower guard...

The Tower guard presents arms, the Chief Warder calls 'God preserve Queen Elizabeth!', the last post is sounded and the keys are entrusted to the Governor for the night.

Richmond Palace
Gallantry on the Green

This palace was originally called Shene Palace. It stood grandly on the banks of the Thames between Richmond and Kew. The young Henry VIII, disguised as a Stranger Knight, fought his first tournament here, probably on Richmond Green.

Richmond as it was in the 17th century...

RICHMOND PALACE

Like most royal palaces, Richmond had its ups and downs.

> **Ups and Downs of Richmond**
> EDWARD III ~ enlarged it.
> RICHARD II ~ wanted to destroy it.
> HENRY V ~ repaired it.
> HENRY VII ~ hid hoards of gold in it.
> HENRY VIII ~ was brought up in it.
> ELIZABETH I ~ died in it (on a huge pile of cushions)
> JAMES I ~ neglected it.
> CHARLES II ~ gave it to his mother (who didn't like it).

And so the palace slowly crumbled. All that is left today is the gateway on Richmond Green, which bears the coat of arms of Henry VII.

Windsor Castle
Garters and Gruesome Drains

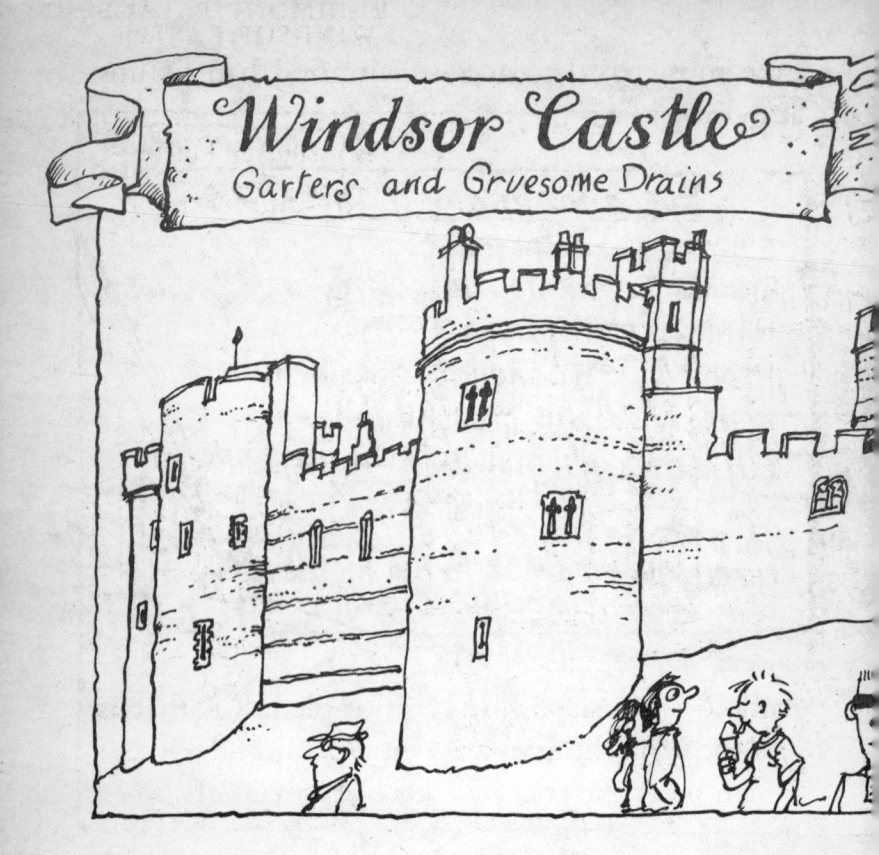

William the Conqueror built the first castle at Windsor. It was probably a large wooden tower on top of a mound, surrounded by a stockade. It was one of a number of fortifications he built in the countryside surrounding London.

100 years later, Henry II began rebuilding the castle in stone. Edward III was born at Windsor, and during his life he improved the royal living-quarters. In 1365, 500 oak trees

WINDSOR CASTLE

Windsor Castle today

were cut down to supply floors and roofs for the palace. Carpenters and stonemasons were brought from all over England to work on the building.

Other monarchs added to the castle. In fact, most of the palace buildings were redesigned no more than 170 years ago. Even the height of the great Round Tower was doubled during George IV's reign.

THE PUFFIN BOOK OF ROYAL LONDON

In 1344, Edward III called a group of chivalrous and brave knights together at Windsor. They were to gather at a Round Table – rather like the knights in the legend of King Arthur. Wars stopped this idea, though the table was built and now hangs in Winchester Castle.

During a dance a few years later, a lady accidentally dropped a garter. The King noticed the smirks on the faces of the courtiers so he picked up the garter, tied it round his own leg and said ...

WINDSOR CASTLE

And thus he founded the 'Most Noble and Amiable Order of St George named the Garter.' Besides the monarch and his or her family, twenty-five others were allowed the honour of the garter.

The Garter Ceremony is still held today. Each Knight of the Garter has a stall in the chapel at Windsor.

Pattern ceiling George's from the of Saint Chapel

Elizabeth I found the castle too cold in winter, though she liked to walk briskly on the battlements before breakfast. Charles II enjoyed staying here, as did Queen Anne.

THE PUFFIN BOOK OF ROYAL LONDON

George III loved Windsor and was known as Farmer George because of his love of the countryside and his interest in farming. He used to stand in the park and watch the local children playing cricket or flying kites.

WINDSOR CASTLE

The living-quarters of the castle were much improved at the beginning of the nineteenth century, but Queen Victoria wasn't really keen on Windsor, though her husband Albert enjoyed it there. However, the ancient and inefficient drains were thought to be the cause of Prince Albert's bout of typhoid which killed him in 1861.

Victoria never really recovered from this shock. Albert's clothes and hot water were brought to his room every day as though he had never died. The glass he sipped his last medicine from lay on the table by his bed for forty years.

The royal family still come to stay at Windsor Castle, making it the only royal palace that has been in use since the Middle Ages.

A bed for guests at Windsor

A Spot of Sport
The Royal Parks

Monarchs and their courtiers loved hunting as a sport. It was a chance to show off their fine clothes and their skills at horsemanship and shooting. There were picnics in the woods during the chase and, of course, banquets at night with wild boar and venison.

A SPOT OF SPORT

Almost every palace had a large hunting-park nearby. Henry VIII used to enjoy hunting on the Black Heath near Greenwich. When Queen Anne grew too ill to ride on horseback, she used to follow the game in a one-horse chaise. She had the parkland at Hampton Court levelled and avenues cleared through the trees. She would then race after stags at a furious pace, mile after mile.

Hyde, St James's, Green and Regent's Parks are all royal parks and are the property of the monarch.

St James's is the oldest royal park. It was once used for hunting, as well as other pastimes. James I had a small zoo here and also an aviary, which stood roughly where Bird Cage Walk is now. Just as today, government officials used to come and sun themselves on summer days.

Samuel Pepys, the famous diary-writer, once wrote that he saw people skating on the frozen lake in winter – the first time he had ever seen the sport.

Charles I walked across the park to his execution at Whitehall. Charles II used to swim in the lake, where there were all types of birds, including pelicans and a crane with a wooden leg.

Hyde Park was one of Henry VIII's favourite hunting-grounds. James I put a wall round it, and it later became a place for fashionable people to stroll and ride in their carriages. It must have been an unusual sight to see servants and coachmen in powdered wigs, beautiful ladies in lace and silk and gentlemen in plumed hats walking among the herds of cows and sheep that were kept in the park.

A SPOT OF SPORT

Samuel Pepys joined these fashionable people once, hoping to catch the eye of the King. He dressed in the latest fashion, including fancy gloves, and hired a horse. Unfortunately, the horse was too frisky and the terrified Pepys had to abandon his plan.

Hyde Park has always been a place of entertainment. There were coach-races, firework displays and fairgrounds.

To celebrate the Battle of Trafalgar, a naval battle was once fought on the Serpentine Lake.

In 1851, Queen Victoria opened the Great Exhibition which took place in the Crystal Palace – an enormous pavilion of glass which sat in the south-east corner of the park.

The story goes that when Queen Victoria asked the Duke of Wellington what could be done about the sparrows that were making a nuisance of themselves in the Crystal Palace, Wellington replied simply...

Sparrow-hawks, Ma'am

Green Park was a favourite haunt of highwaymen, duellists and balloonists. In the middle of the nineteenth century, a Mr Green filled his balloon from a Piccadilly gas-main and floated off from the park (he made 527 ascents during his life).

Charles II built a 'snow house' in the park for keeping ice to cool drinks in the summer. The mound of the snow house can still be seen.

Regent's Park was once part of a great forest and another favourite royal hunting-ground. A survey at the end of Charles I's reign showed there were just over 16,000 trees in the park. Soon most of them were chopped down and the park turned into farmland.

Henry VIII was probably the most athletic monarch. Among other sports, he liked wrestling, archery and tennis. There were tennis-courts at Greenwich and Hampton Court – the one at Hampton Court is still in use.

A SPOT OF SPORT

Charles II was also a keen tennis player. He used to weigh himself before and after every game to see how much weight he had lost.

Charles II also played Pell Mell in which a ball was hit through an iron hoop with a wooden mallet (a bit like croquet). The game was played in St James's Park and the street which is today called Pall Mall is probably roughly where the competitors stood.

Greenwich Palace
Ships and Puddles

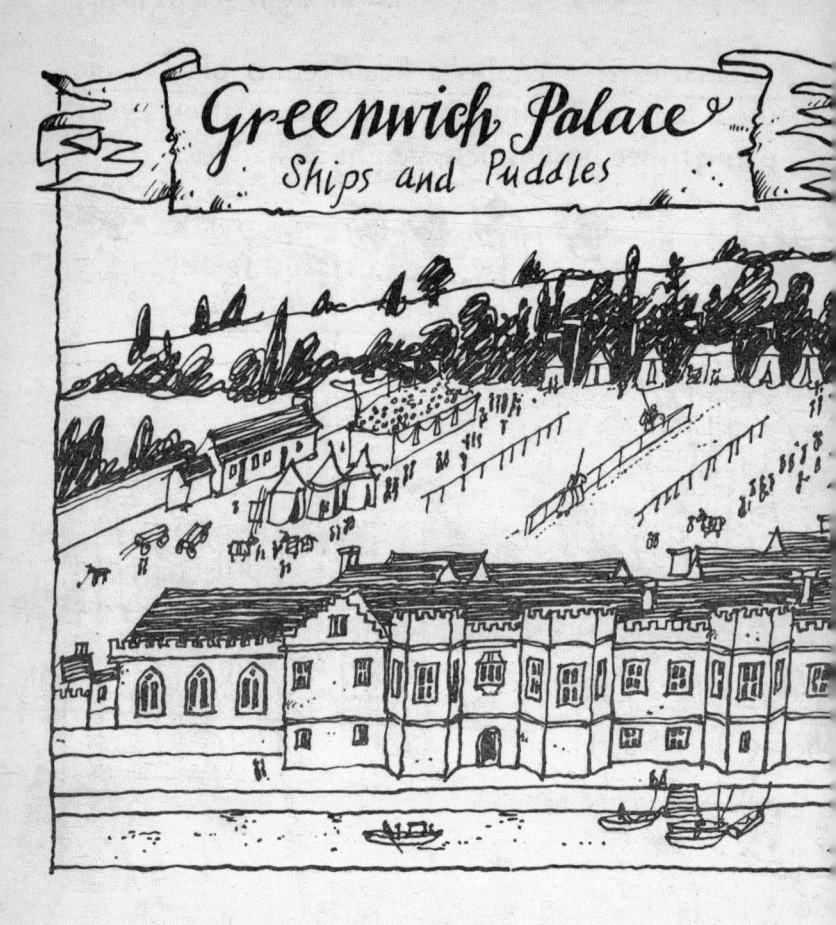

The original house was built by the Duke of Gloucester in 1427 and named Bella Court. The next occupants were Henry VI and his wife Margaret of Anjou, who renamed the house 'Placentia', or pleasant place. She decorated the rooms of the palace and added glass to the windows.

GREENWICH PALACE

Greenwich in Henry VIII's reign with a joust taking place in the lists.

Henry VIII was born here, as were his daughters, Mary and Elizabeth. It was Henry's favourite palace and he enlarged it until it was an impressive building with courtyards, a banqueting hall, lawns, fountains and orchards.

THE PUFFIN BOOK OF ROYAL LONDON

Incidents at Greenwich

For some time, Henry VIII had heard gossip about his second wife, Anne Boleyn. He was jealous that she was spending too much time in the company of other men of the court.

Oh, hooray! Hooray, Sir Harry!

During a jousting tournament, Anne seemed to cheer the King's groom, Sir Harry Norris, a little too eagerly. Henry left the joust abruptly, and the next day Anne was conveyed to the Tower to await interrogation and execution, accused of being an unfaithful wife.

GREENWICH PALACE

Once, when Mary I was staying at the palace, a cannon-ball that had been fired in salute came crashing through the room where she was sitting. No one was injured, but they were more than a little disturbed!

The palace was in a good position to watch the comings and goings of ships on the River Thames. Merchant ships from abroad passed the windows with silks and spices and wine. Warships were built at nearby Deptford and Woolwich.

THE PUFFIN BOOK OF ROYAL LONDON

On the other hand, when the Spanish Armada set sail for Britain, it was decided the palace was well within reach of the enemy ships. Queen Elizabeth I quickly moved her court to safer St James's.

In 1576, Martin Frobisher set sail on a voyage of exploration to America, and Queen Elizabeth waved her farewells from a window.

Four years later, the Queen saw the return of Francis Drake after one of the first round-the-world voyages. She knighted Drake aboard his ship, the *Golden Hind*, which was later moored at Greenwich (like the *Cutty Sark*) for Londoners to visit.

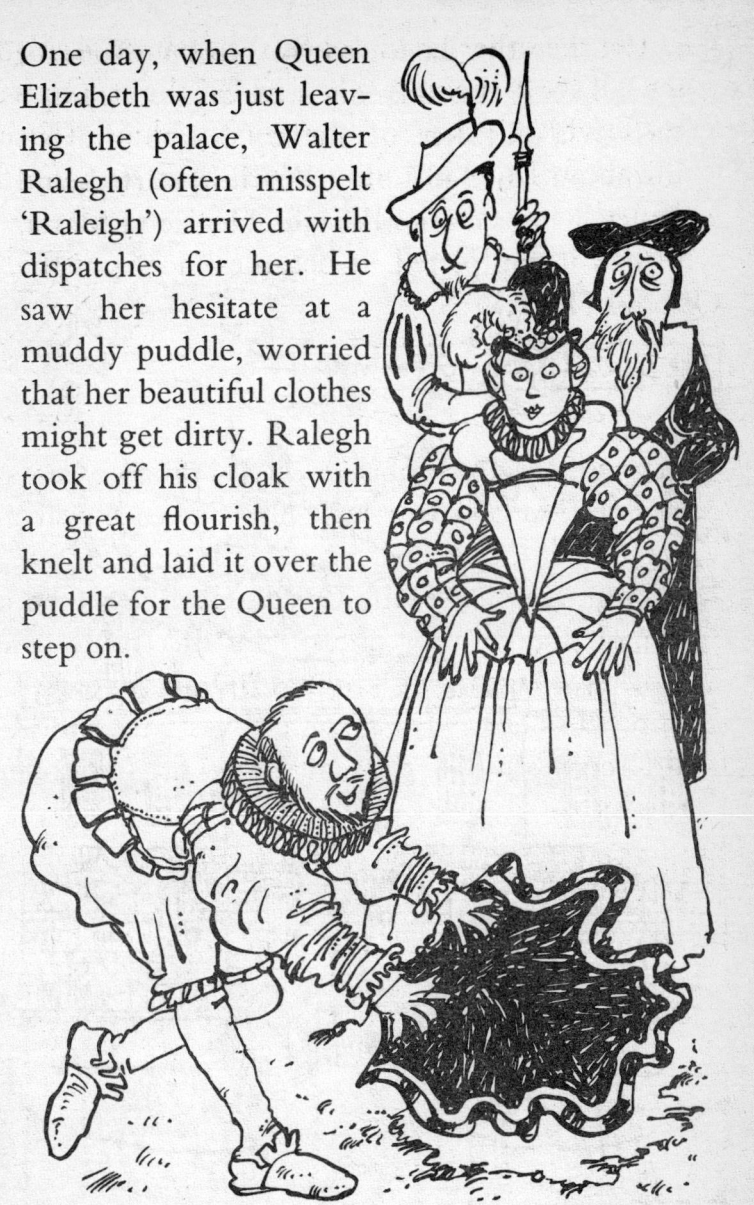

GREENWICH PALACE

One day, when Queen Elizabeth was just leaving the palace, Walter Ralegh (often misspelt 'Raleigh') arrived with dispatches for her. He saw her hesitate at a muddy puddle, worried that her beautiful clothes might get dirty. Ralegh took off his cloak with a great flourish, then knelt and laid it over the puddle for the Queen to step on.

James I gave the palace to his Queen, Anne of Denmark. She commissioned the architect, Inigo Jones, to build her a smaller palace nearby. Queen Anne died just after building started, and so it was King Charles I's wife, Henrietta Maria, who had it completed. It became known as the Queen's House.

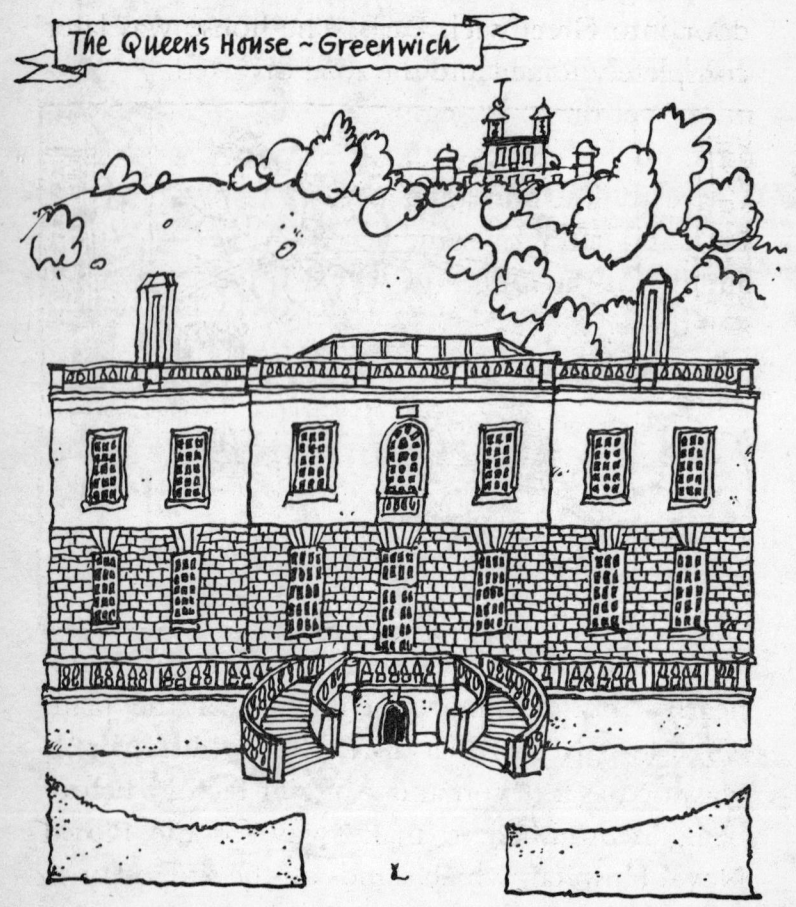

The Queen's House ~ Greenwich

GREENWICH PALACE

Oddly enough, it was built over the main road from Deptford to Woolwich. As this was a public pathway it could not be blocked, so half of the house was built on one side of the road and half on the other, and it was connected by a bridge. The Queen could step out of one door into the grounds of Placentia or step out of another door into Greenwich Park. The house was later completely joined and the road diverted.

King Charles II decided to build a 'King's House' nearby, but nothing much came of the plan. The old palace of Placentia fell into disrepair. It was used as a prison and a biscuit factory before being demolished to make way for the Royal Naval Hospital, which stands on the site today.

Flutes and Fireworks
Music at Court

The rooms and halls of the palaces often rang with the sound of music. Most monarchs could play a musical instrument, anything from the lute (Henry VIII) to the piano (Victoria, who played duets with her husband, Albert).

Henry VIII had an orchestra called the 'Kinge's Musicke', and there were numerous instruments in each of his palaces, as can be seen from inventories.

Inventory of instruments of musicke in the Palaces of His Majesty Henry VIII :-

GREENWICH - one pair regalles (small organ)

WESTMINSTER - one pair regalles covered in crimson velvet and pearls (+ bellows)
- a pair of clavicords
- 14 viols, great and small
- Flutes
- 6 recorders
- 1 bass recorder
- Bagpipes

HAMPTON CT. - organs and virginalls (7 pairs)

WHITEHALL - Great Organ
one old lute.

FLUTES AND FIREWORKS

The great banqueting halls at the palaces always had a balcony where musicians played while people feasted.

Dancing took place, too, usually after supper. In Elizabeth I's court, the pavan was popular. It was a slow and stately dance so that courtiers who wore long gowns – the lawyers and elderly statesmen, for instance – could join in.

55

The volta was livelier. The gentlemen had to grasp the ladies by the waist and lift them into the air. Gentlemen were advised to remove their swords for this, in case of accidents.

Masques were popular too. These were dramas accompanied by music in which everyone dressed up in elaborate costumes, including the monarch and family.

Sometimes there were just too many people taking part – and too much wine was drunk! At a masque to entertain the King of Denmark at James I's court, a lady playing the part of the Queen of Sheba fell over and dropped a tray of

FLUTES AND FIREWORKS

sweetmeats. They fell on the Danish King's lap. It was too much for the poor King and he was carried away and laid on a bed, his clothes covered in cream, jelly and wine.

Music was often performed out of doors. One balmy summer evening George I took a trip on the river. One newspaper reported...

> **20 JULY　DAILY COURANT　1717**
>
> A city Company's barge was employed for the musicke, wherein were 50 instruments of all sorts who played all the way from Lambeth the finest symphonies composed express for this occasion by MR HANDEL.

That music has become known as Handel's 'Water Music'.

Handel also composed music for a royal firework display (which included 10,000 rockets) in Green Park. The 'Music for the Royal Fireworks' was a success, but the English and Italian firework engineers ended up fighting.

Whitehall Palace — Damp and Draughty

The Banqueting Hall

The King's and Queen's apartm[ents]

Whitehall began life as York Place, the London home of the Archbishops of York. Henry VIII confiscated the palace from Archbishop Thomas Wolsey when Wolsey fell out of favour.

An act of parliament in 1530 stated that all the land from Charing Cross to Westminster was to be known as the King's Palace – quite a large area!

WHITEHALL PALACE

The Palace around the time of Charles II

It seems that the palace was a higgledy-piggledy sort of place – a great sprawl of buildings of all shapes and sizes, set around many courtyards and passageways. Foreign visitors thought it a rather disgraceful place – certainly not a residence fit for a king or queen.

When Henry VIII moved into the palace, he gave it a new name – Whitehall – and added yet more buildings to it. However, he came across a problem. The palace was hemmed in by the river on one side and the main road from Charing Cross to Westminster on the other. Because this was a public thoroughfare, no one was allowed to build on it – not even the King.

The problem was solved by building two elaborate gateways across the road. These carried passageways from the old parts of the palace to the new buildings on the far side of the road.

The Holbein Gate joining two parts of the Palace...

Main road

WHITEHALL PALACE

The only part of Wolsey's original palace that is still standing is the wine-cellar. The whole cellar was moved to one side and sunk 6 metres when the Ministry of Defence building was built on top.

James I decided to rebuild the palace as a house more suitable for a monarch. Two architects, Inigo Jones and John Webb, drew up plans for a huge palace, but only the banqueting house was completed in 1622.

THE PUFFIN BOOK OF ROYAL LONDON

There had been several banqueting houses near this site. The first one was of wood and canvas – like a marquee. Elizabeth I built another wood and canvas structure, but it had glass windows and was beautifully painted with a stonework effect on the outside and clouds, sun and stars on the ceiling inside. A third banqueting house was destroyed by fire. Inigo Jones's hall was praised by visitors who thought it a well-proportioned and elegant building.

James I's son, Charles I, walked out of one of the banqueting house windows on to the platform where he was beheaded in 1649.

WHITEHALL PALACE

By Charles II's time, the palace included an aviary, a chemical laboratory, a theatre and tennis-courts. In 1689, William and Mary were proclaimed King and Queen at Whitehall, but as neither of them liked the place, they moved to Kensington.

The end of the palace came when a maid hung some clothes to dry in front of a fire. The clothes caught alight and most of the palace was burnt down – about 1,000 rooms!

The Banqueting Hall today

Cheers and Chivalry
The Royal Tilt-yards

The joust was a spectacle that everyone could come and watch. It was perhaps one of the few places where ordinary people could catch a glimpse of the monarch. Jousting tournaments were therefore splendid affairs and were meant to create a good impression. The tilt-yards would be filled with the fanfares of trumpets, bright costumes, flags, horses and gleaming armour. The King and Queen would sit in splendour, surrounded by honoured guests, courtiers and viewing-stands crammed with excited spectators.

Prizes were awarded at the banquet after the tournament. The prize would be a jewel or perhaps a kiss from the Lady of the tournament.

CHEERS AND CHIVALRY

There were tilt-yards — where the jousting took place — at all the palaces. The tilt-yard for Westminster lay where the tower of Big Ben stands today. Where buses thunder up Whitehall, there was once the thunder of horses' hoofs!

Before the joust proper began, there were always pageants with decorative floats. At one tournament in 1609, the crowd had some extra amusement. A huge elephant float arrived late — the joust had already started — and bumbled about the tilt-yard, unable to find a way out.

THE PUFFIN BOOK OF ROYAL LONDON

During the tournament, knights charged at each other up either side of a wooden barrier. They tried to break a lance against their opponent's armour.

Arming pavilions

Wire screen to prevent splinters hitting royal box

Barrier

Sword basket

Heralds announced names of knights at start of contest, kept scores and proclaimed winners.

CHEERS AND CHIVALRY

There was also combat on foot with swords and the 'tourney', which was a sort of free-for-all between two teams.

Royal box

Important people

Not so important people

Rebate lances (blunted for safety)

Score cards were kept. Points were deducted for fouls, e.g. striking opponent's horse. The strokes in the box are the number of hits scored. The strokes outside are the number of courses run.

Edward Topstrike

Percy Goodblow

Lance stand

Hampton Court Palace
Marvels and Mazes

Hampton Court was one of the grandest palaces. It was built by Cardinal Wolsey when he became Lord Chancellor of England. He felt that, as Henry VIII's chief minister, a magnificent palace would create a good impression at home and abroad.

HAMPTON COURT PALACE

The west front and Great Gatehouse

Before building started, Wolsey took advice from his doctors, who proclaimed the site very good for the health. Some of the stone for the building was brought from as far away as France, and miles of pipe brought fresh water from distant hills.

The Venetian ambassador once said with great awe that he had to pass through no less than eight rooms before arriving at Wolsey's private chamber. Each room was hung with tapestries and the tapestries were changed once a week.

How much further?

Only another 20 rooms

When Wolsey fell out of favour with the King, he offered him his palace as a gift. Henry took it, but it didn't save Wolsey – remember he lost York Place too!

Henry added much to the palace. For banquets he built a great hall with a musicians' gallery. He added kitchens, wine-cellars, pantries, a tennis-court and a tilt-yard. He spent so much money on entertainments that Thomas Cromwell (Wolsey's replacement) grew worried about the King's spendthrift lifestyle.

HAMPTON COURT PALACE

Queen Mary I spent her honeymoon with her husband, Philip of Spain, at Hampton Court. She died childless, so was succeeded by her sister, Elizabeth.

Elizabeth I's lifestyle at Hampton Court was every bit as lavish as her father's. People talked of seeing tapestries gleaming with pearls, rooms dazzling with diamonds, gold, silver and glass. The place was filled with music and the Queen would recline on silk cushions, wearing one of her 3,000 dresses.

In the Clock Court there is the famous clock made by the 'Deviser of the King's Horologies' for Henry VIII. It tells the time, the month, the day, number of days since the start of the year, phases of the moon, astrological signs and important travel information — the times of the high tides.

The large gardens changed over the years according to the taste of the monarch. Elizabeth I enjoyed working in the garden herself. Explorers brought exotic plants from abroad – like the potato and tobacco plants. William III made parterres (flower-beds surrounded by low hedges of box-plants). Queen Anne didn't like the smell of box, so she replaced the flower-beds with broad lawns and clipped yew trees. The famous maze was planted about this time and there is a Great Vine which is almost 200 years old.

James I bought many paintings for the rooms and invited troupes of comedians and actors (including Shakespeare) to perform for him at court.

In Oliver Cromwell's time, there was a call for the palace to be demolished. It survived, but some items were sold – Henry VIII's walking-stick fetched five shillings.

HAMPTON COURT PALACE

William and Mary decided to spend some time at Hampton Court. They commissioned the architect Sir Christopher Wren to redesign the palace. Although he was busy building St Paul's Cathedral, he set to work. Wren cleverly added new buildings round the old palace, giving the impression that it was an entirely new building. He made the palace look rather grand, and by this time it was surrounded by long avenues of trees, lakes and fountains.

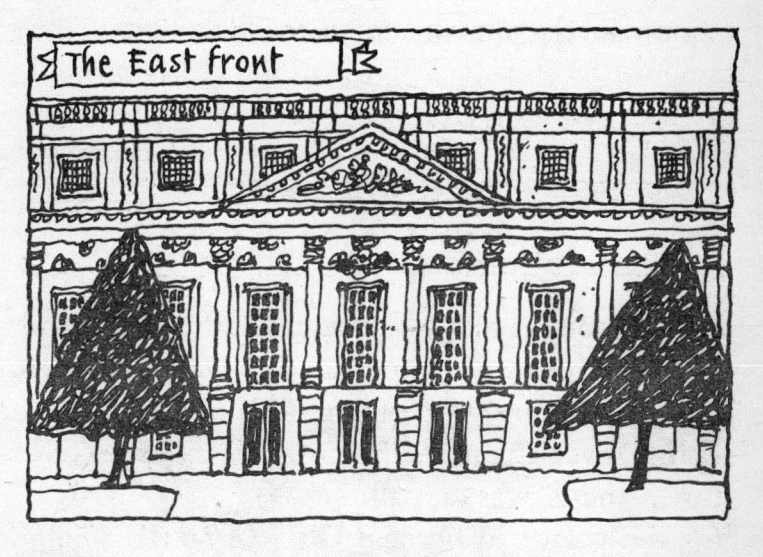

The East front

After William and Mary, monarchs spent little time at the palace. During Queen Victoria's reign the palace was restored and became a favourite place for Londoners to visit when a railway-station was built nearby in 1849.

All Glass and Gilt
The Royal Coaches

For centuries the only way to travel long distances was on horseback. Kings and queens travelled this way too, because coaches did not appear on the streets until the middle of the sixteenth century. Queen Mary I and Queen Elizabeth I were the first monarchs to make use of coaches. Today, the present Queen travels in a coach to certain royal events, even long after the invention of cars!

The Scottish State Coach

ALL GLASS AND GILT

Queen Elizabeth I being carried on a litter during a Royal Progress.

75

Today the coaches are housed in the Royal Mews. The mews were places where the Royal Falcons were kept. Later, the name was used for the Royal Kennels and Stables.

Above: a State Landau
Below: The Gold State Coach, built in 1762. It weighs 4 tonnes, is pulled by eight horses and is used at coronations.

Kensington Palace
Highwaymen and Wild Boys

William III and his wife Mary didn't like Whitehall Palace. The dampness from the river and the smoke from the city troubled William's asthma. After looking around for somewhere more suitable to live, they bought Nottingham House in the village of Kensington, which in those days was outside the city of London.

Sir Christopher Wren was appointed to enlarge

KENSINGTON PALACE

and improve the house, now called Kensington Palace. Queen Mary was so keen to have the place completed that she visited the site and urged the workmen to hurry up. Just after her visit, some scaffolding fell down and workmen were injured. Mary was very embarrassed because she felt that her nagging was partly the cause of the accident.

Queen Anne redesigned the gardens and built an orangery where oranges, lemons and other exotic plants could be grown. She held supper parties amid the scented blossoms. She is said to have died here of a fit of apoplexy due to over-eating.

A long straight road was laid from the new palace into London. It was called the Route du Roi – the King's Way – but the name has been changed to Rotten Row over the years. It was lit all the way by lamps – the first street to have street-lighting. This was to try and prevent robberies by the highwaymen that lurked around these parts.

KENSINGTON PALACE

George I had additions made to the palace, as well as installing paintings for the King's Grand Staircase. The walls were painted to look like balconies, with people glancing down as if welcoming the King. These people included Mustapha and Mahomet, two Turkish servants, Christian Ulrich Jorry, the royal dwarf, and Peter the Wild Boy, who was found living wild in the woods of Germany, walking on all fours like an animal.

George II died in his water-closet (loo) at the palace, and thereafter, monarchs preferred to live elsewhere.

But another very important person was born and brought up in the palace. In 1819 the Duchess of Kent gave birth to a daughter. At her christening her uncle, the Prince Regent, made her mother cry by disagreeing with the choice of names.

Victoria lived in a small suite of rooms, where she had to share a bedroom with her mother. The only other people in this part of the palace were Victoria's strict tutor, the Baroness Lehzen, and a royal attendant, Sir John Conroy.

At dawn on 20 June 1837, the Lord Chamberlain and the Archbishop of Canterbury arrived hurriedly at the palace. They had come to announce to Victoria that William IV had died and she was now Queen.

A month later Victoria left what she called 'the poor old palace' to move into Buckingham Palace.

Towser and the Lions
Some Royal Beasts

Animals were often given as gifts from one monarch to another. There was a royal menagerie in the Tower of London in Henry III's time.

The king had three leopards which had been presented to him by Emperor Frederick II. There were also several lions – Marco, Phyllis and their son, Nero. There was once a quartet of lions with rather confusing names – Fanny, Miss Fanny, Miss Fanny Howe and Miss Howe.

Henry III also received a polar bear (plus its keeper) from the King of Norway. The bear was allowed to hunt for fish in the Thames on the end of a long rope.

A few years later there came a gift from the King of France – an elephant. This was the first elephant to be seen in Britain and was quite an attraction.

Decorative beasts from Hampton Court.

Other animals included a panther, tigers, bears, owls, a racoon, a porcupine, monkeys, vultures and hyenas.

Unfortunately, the animals weren't kept in very good condition and dogs were sometimes set upon the lions and bears in the sport of baiting.

In 1834 the animals were moved to the new Zoological Gardens in Regent's Park.

Most of the monarchs kept dogs. Charles I's little dog accompanied him across St James's Park on the way to his execution.

TOWSER AND THE LIONS

Charles II had many dogs. It is said that at official meetings of state, he preferred playing with his dogs rather than listening to what was being discussed.

When he had a new bedroom built at Whitehall Palace, there had to be special cushions for the dogs and a wire screen round his bed to stop the dogs spoiling it.

When he lost one of his dogs in the park, he put an advert in the *London Gazette* . . .

LOST DOG

£5 REWARD for return of liver~colour'd and white~spotted spaniel answering to the name of TOWSER

contact Palace

St James's Palace
Wear the Right Wig

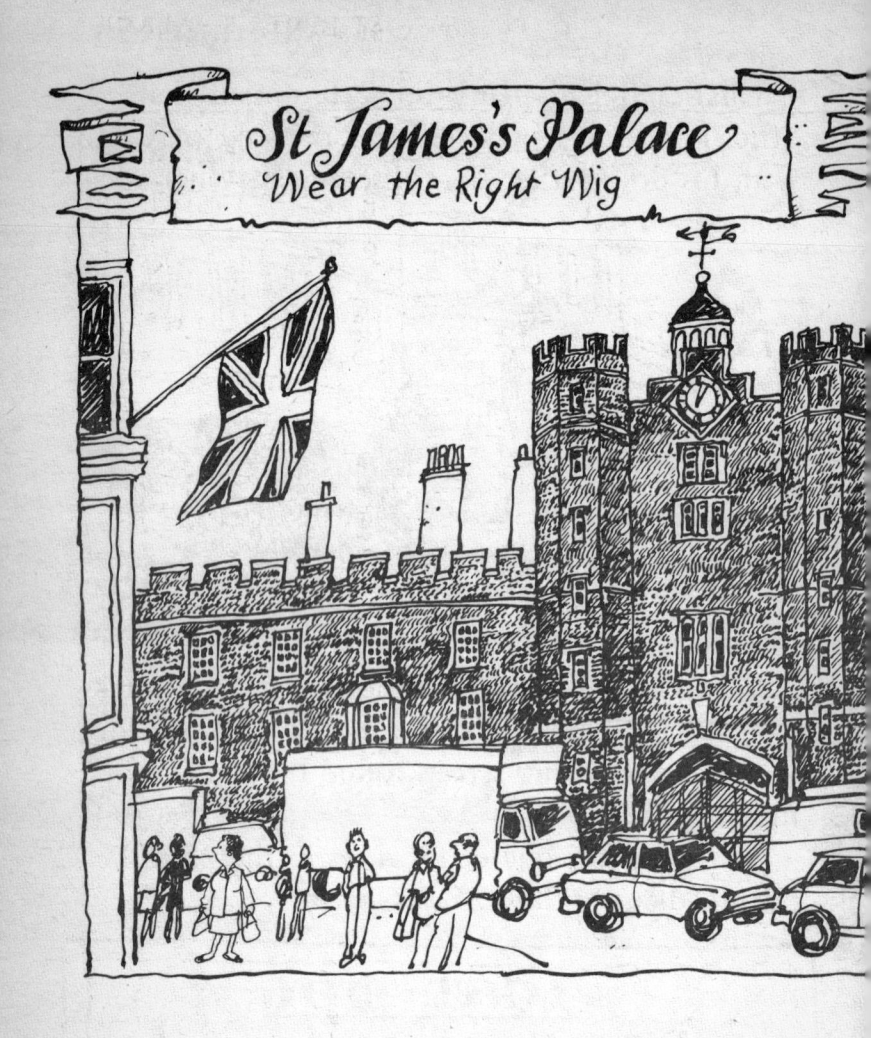

St James's is a shy palace that huddles almost unseen behind the traffic of the London streets. It was built by Henry VIII and was lived in, from time to time, by many monarchs.

Queen Mary I liked it. Once a man tried to

ST JAMES'S PALACE

assassinate her by burning her to a crisp. He climbed up on to the roof of the palace and held up a burning-glass (large lens) to focus the sun's rays on the Queen as she walked in the park below. He was unsuccessful.

The palace wasn't grand enough for Elizabeth I. James I gave it to his eldest son, Henry, who set up a swear-box in the palace. Anyone heard swearing had to put money in the box, which was later given to the poor.

Queen Anne made it her official residence, but life at her court was extremely dull. When in conversation with strangers, she talked only about the weather.

ST JAMES'S PALACE

No one was allowed to smoke a pipe or wear spectacles. Those not wearing a proper wig were sent home to change.

By Queen Anne's reign, St James's Park outside the palace had been tidied up and avenues of trees planted. The Queen was very annoyed when the Duke of Buckingham rebuilt his house at the other end of the park, making it look as if the park belonged to him. In the future, this house would become Buckingham Palace.

Though Queen Victoria and Prince Albert were married in the palace, it was not their home.

Although the present Queen officially lives at Buckingham Palace, ambassadors from foreign countries are still called 'Ambassador to the Court of St James's'.

Salt and Sweetmeats
Royal Meals

Court banquets, like palaces and jousts, were used to show off the monarch's wealth and hospitality to foreign guests.

As thousands of meals had to be made every day, the palaces had huge kitchens, as well as larders, pantries, wine-cellars and bake-houses. The Clerk of the Kitchen was in charge of all this at Henry VIII's court. Under him were all sorts of officers, from the Sergeant of the Larder and the Chief Clerk of the Spicery to the Yeomen of the Mouth (the waiters).

Even the laying of the table was a great ceremony. Once the tablecloth had been put on, the Great Salt (salt cellar) was always the first item to be placed in the middle of the table. The Lady Taster then gave morsels of food to the guards on duty – to make sure none of it was poisoned!

SALT AND SWEETMEATS

In Charles II's time, ice-cream became popular and ice-houses were made to store ice during the summer. These were deep underground pits, filled in winter with ice and snow.

The word 'banquet' originally meant a table of sweetmeats. When William and Mary entertained the Venetian ambassadors, the sweetmeats were piled so high that no one could see across the table and the guests were terrified of touching them.

For centuries, honoured citizens were allowed in to watch the monarch dine. George II was more business-like about it – tickets were sold to the public to watch the King and Queen at their lunch.

Buckingham Palace
No silkworms or sinks

Buckingham House stood in a place called the Mulberry Garden. It was called this ever since James I planted mulberry trees to try and improve the silk industry (silkworms eat mulberry leaves). The wrong type of trees were planted so the worms died. The house was regarded as one of the most beautiful buildings in London and many monarchs cast jealous eyes on it. It was eventually bought by George III, but it was

BUCKINGHAM PALACE

George IV who enlarged it into a palace.

The government voted to give the king some money to improve the house, but in the end much more money was required because of the costly materials that were used, including hundreds of blocks of Carrara marble from Italy. The palace was built round three sides of a courtyard, with an imposing marble arch at its entrance.

King George didn't live to see his palace finished and the next monarch, his brother William IV, never lived in it either. He didn't much like the place. He offered it to the government as a new house of parliament, as the old one had just recently burnt down. He even thought of turning it into an army barracks. Other people disliked it too. After a politician, Thomas Creevey, had been shown round, he said...

It's so vulgar it ought to be called the Brunswick Hotel.

Queen Victoria was the first monarch to live in it and she moved in eagerly. Soon the impressive rooms were filled with balls and banquets and important visitors.

However, when she first arrived the drains were faulty, there were no sinks for the maids, the lavatories were unventilated, the bells wouldn't ring, the doors wouldn't close and the windows wouldn't open!

BUCKINGHAM PALACE

Some years later, the courtyard was closed off by another wing and the marble arch was moved to where it now stands, at the end of Oxford Street.

Edward VII had the front of the palace redesigned, and the palace remains the official London residence of the present Queen, Elizabeth II.

Handy List of Monarchs
A who's who of Palace tenants

EDWARD THE CONFESSOR 1042–1066	HAROLD II 1066	WILLIAM I (THE CONQUEROR) 1066–1087	WILLIAM II (RUFUS) 1087–1100
HENRY I 1100–1135	STEPHEN 1135–1154	HENRY II 1154–1189	RICHARD I 1189–1199

HANDY LIST OF MONARCHS

JOHN 1199–1216	HENRY III 1216–1272	EDWARD I 1272–1307	EDWARD II 1307–1327
EDWARD III 1327–1377	RICHARD II 1377–1399	HENRY IV 1399–1413	HENRY V 1413–1422
HENRY VI 1422–1461 and 1470–1471	EDWARD IV 1461–1470 and 1471–1483	EDWARD V 1483	RICHARD III 1483–1485

THE PUFFIN BOOK OF ROYAL LONDON

HENRY VII 1485–1509	HENRY VIII 1509–1547	EDWARD VI 1547–1553	MARY I 1553–1558
ELIZABETH I 1558–1603	(At this point James VI of Scotland became James I of Scotland and England)	JAMES I 1603–1625	CHARLES I 1625–1649

PROTECTOR OLIVER CROMWELL 1649–1660

CHARLES II 1660–1685	JAMES II 1685–1688	WILLIAM III & MARY II 1689–1702 1689–1694

HANDY LIST OF MONARCHS

ANNE 1702–1714	GEORGE I 1714–1727	GEORGE II 1727–1760	GEORGE III 1760–1820
GEORGE IV 1820–1830	WILLIAM IV 1830–1837	VICTORIA 1837–1901	EDWARD VII 1901–1910
GEORGE V 1910–1936	EDWARD VIII 1936	GEORGE VI 1936–1952	ELIZABETH II 1952–

Ghosts

It is said that the ghost of Henry VIII's fifth wife, the unfortunate Catherine Howard (beheaded), can sometimes be seen running wildly through the rooms of Hampton Court.

At the Tower, the list of ghosts is endless – mysteriously coloured human figures, crying babies, eerie footsteps, screams, headless corpses, etc.

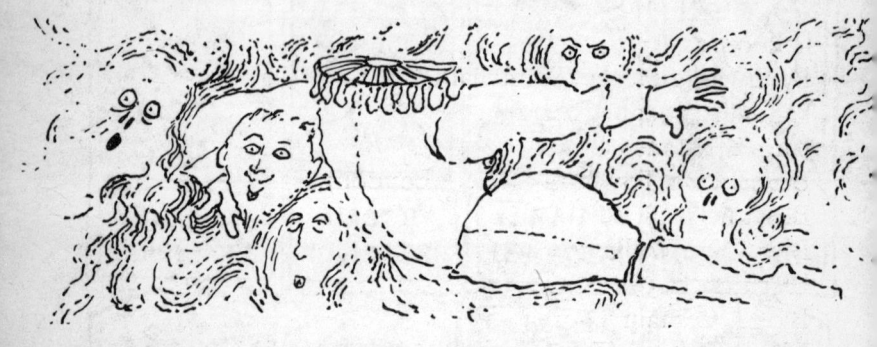

Whether you believe in all this or not, it would be difficult to find a group of homes so filled with events and memories – both joyful and sad – as the royal palaces.

The good thing is that most of them are open to the public and we can all go and spend an hour or two sampling their colourful history. Anyone for the rack?

Index

Albert, Prince Consort, 3, 13, 37
animals, 83–5
Anne, Queen, 2, 35, 39, 72
   at Kensington Palace, 80
   at St James's Palace, 88–9
Anne of Denmark, 52
aviaries, 39, 63

balloonists, 43
Banqueting House (Whitehall), 61–2
banquets, at court, 7, 90–91
barges, 11, 12–13
Beauchamp Tower (Tower of London), 17
Beefeaters, 18, 29
Bird Cage Walk, 39
Blackheath, 39
Blood, Captain Thomas, 27–8
Bloody Tower (Tower of London), 17, 29
Boleyn, Anne, 12, 25, 48
Bowyer Tower (Tower of London), 17
Buckingham Palace, 3, 82, 89, 92–5

Ceremony of the Keys, 29
Chapel of the Pyx (Westminster Palace), 8
Charles I, 40, 62, 84
Charles II, 12, 16, 26, 31, 35, 43, 53
   dogs of, 85

in St James's Park, 40
  playing sports, 45
Clarence, George, Duke of, 17
Clerk of the Kitchen, 90
Clock Court (Hampton Court), 71
coaches, 74–7
coronations, 12, 16
Creevey, Thomas, 94
Cromwell, Oliver, 7
Cromwell, Thomas, 70
crown jewels, 26–8
Crystal Palace, 42

dancing, at royal courts, 55–6
Deptford, 49
dogs, 84–5
drains, 3, 37
Drake, Francis, 50

Edward the Confessor, 5
Edward III, 31, 32, 34
Edward V, 22
Edward VII, 95
Edward VIII, 3
Edwards, Talbot, 26–7
elephants, 84
Elizabeth I, 22, 31, 35, 47, 74, 75, 88
  explorers and, 50–51
  at Hampton Court, 71–2
  and Whitehall, 62
Elizabeth II, 89, 95
executions, 24–5

Fawkes, Guy, 23

INDEX

fireworks, 57
Flambard, Ranulf, Bishop of Durham, 23
Frederick, Prince of Wales (1707–51), 13
Frobisher, Martin, 50

gardens
   at Hampton Court, 72
   at Kensington Palace, 80
Garter, Knights of, 34
George I, 57, 81
George II, 81, 91
George III, 2, 36, 92
George IV, 82, 93–4
ghosts, 100
Golden Hind, 50
graffiti, 17
Great Exhibition, 1851, 42
Great Hall (Westminster Hall), 6, 10
Green Park, 43, 57
Greenwich Palace, 2, 44, 46–9, 54
Gundulf, Bishop of Rochester, 15

Hampton Court, 2, 39, 44, 54, 68–73, 100
Handel, George Frederick, 57
Henrietta Maria, Queen, 52
Henry II, 32
Henry III, 83–4
Henry V, 31
Henry VI, 46
Henry VII, 31
Henry VIII, 39, 40, 44, 48, 86
   at Greenwich Palace, 2, 47
   at Hampton Court, 70
   music and, 54

at Richmond Palace, 30, 31
　　　at Whitehall Palace, 58, 60
Henry Frederick, Prince of Wales (1594–1612), 88
highwaymen, 80
Holbein Gate (Whitehall), 60
Houses of Parliament, 10
Howard, Catherine, 25, 100
Howard, Lady Frances, 22
hunting, 38–9, 44
Hyde Park, 40–42

ice houses, 43, 91

James I, 31, 39, 40, 52, 88, 92
　　at Hampton Court, 72
　　at Whitehall Palace, 61
Jewel Tower (Westminster Palace), 9, 10
Jones, Inigo, 52, 61
jousting, 64–7

Kensington Palace, 78–82
Kinge's Musicke, 54
kings and queens, list of, 96–9

Lady Taster, 90

Marble Arch, 95
Margaret of Anjou, 46
Martin Tower (Tower of London), 26, 28
Mary I, 2, 22, 71, 74
　　at Greenwich, 47, 49
　　at St James's Palace, 86–7
Mary II, 3, 63, 78, 79, 91
masques, 56–7

INDEX

maze, at Hampton Court, 72
Mulberry Gardens, 92
music, at court, 54–7

Nithsdale, William Maxwell, 5th Earl of, 23
Norris, Sir Harry, 48

Order of the Garter, 35
Overbury, Sir Thomas, 22

pageants, 65
paintings, 81
palaces, 1–3: *see also* names of individual palaces
Pall Mall, 45
parks, 38–45
pell mell, 45
Pepys, Samuel, 40, 41
Placentia (Greenwich Palace), 46, 53
Podlicote, Richard de, 8
Princes in the Tower, 22
prisoners, in the Tower of London, 17, 18, 20–23

Queen's House, Greenwich, 52–3

Ralegh, Walter, 51
ravens, in the Tower of London, 19
Regent's Park, 44
Richard II, 6, 31
Richard III, 22
Richmond Palace, 30–31
Rotten Row, 80
Round Table, 34
Royal Armouries Museum, 16
Royal Mews, 76

Royal Mint, 14
Royal Naval Hospital, Greenwich, 53
royal parks, 38–45
Royal Treasury (Westminster Palace), 8

St James's Palace, 2, 86–9
St James's Park, 39–40, 45, 89
Serpentine Lake, 41
ships, 49–50
Shene Palace (Richmond Palace), 30
Somerset, Duchess of, 23
Somerset House, 13
Spanish Armada, 50
swearing, at court, 88

tapestries, 70, 71
tennis, 44, 45, 63, 70
Thames, River, 7, 11–13, 49
tilt-yards, 64–5, 70
torture, 21
Tower of London, 14–21, 29, 83
  crown jewels in, 26–8
  executions at, 24–5
  ghosts of, 100
Traitor's Gate, 20
treason, 24
treasure, 8

Ussheborne, William, 9

Victoria, Queen, 37, 54, 89, 94
  birth of, 82
  at Great Exhibition, 42

INDEX

Wakefield Tower (Tower of London), 19
Webb, John, 61
Wellington, Arthur Wellesley, Duke of, 42
Westminster Hall, 6, 10
Westminster Palace, 5–10, 54
White Tower (Tower of London), 15, 16
Whitehall (street), 65
Whitehall Palace, 3, 54, 58–63
wigs, 89
William I (the Conqueror), 32
William II (Rufus), 6
William III, 3, 63, 72, 73, 78, 91
William IV, 94
Windsor Castle, 3, 32–7
Wolsey, Thomas, 58, 68, 69, 70
Woolwich, 13, 49
Wren, Sir Christopher, 73, 78

Yeoman Gaoler, 18
Yeoman Warders, 18, 29
York Place (Whitehall Palace), 58

zoos
    in Regent's Park (London Zoo), 84
    in St James's Park, 39
    at the Tower of London, 14

Also in Puffin

ENVIRONMENTALLY YOURS
Early Times

What is the greenhouse effect? Why is the Earth getting warmer? Who is responsible for the destruction of the countryside? Where can you get advice on recycling? When will the Earth's resources run out? The answers to all these questions and many more are given in this forthright and informative book. Topics such as transport, industry, agriculture, population and energy are covered as well as lists of 'green' organizations and useful addresses.

ANIMAL KIND
Early Times

Animal Kind looks at what humans are doing to animals. It also looks at what humans *could* be doing for animals to make their lives happier and to lessen their suffering. This is a hard-hitting book that covers topics such as vivisection, vegetarianism, farming, wildlife, pets and blood sports. It will help you look again at your relationship to the animal world.

DEAR JO
Early Times

Have *you* ever had a real problem like falling out with your best friend; not being able to read properly because of dyslexia; feeling lonely and unloved because your parents have separated; being hooked on *Neighbours* and not able to think of anything else?

Well, maybe you're not alone! Lots of others feel the same way and many of them ask for help by writing to advice columnists like Jo in the *Early Times*. Just telling someone else about your problems can make things better, and getting a helpful, kind and often funny letter back can soon put a smile back on the glummest of faces!

In this book you'll find the answers to lots of problems you may have had, or are likely to have while you're growing up. Some are serious, some more light-hearted – so have a good read, a bit of a giggle and *do* stop worrying!

THE *EARLY TIMES* BOOK OF CROSSWORDS

There are TV and radio puzzles, Hallowe'en puzzles, skeleton puzzles, science puzzles as well as straightforward crossword puzzles to keep you going for hours, days, weeks, months – in fact, as long as your brain can stand it. Whether you're a beginner or an addict, this book of crosswords from the *Early Times* will make you think and keep you puzzling.

WAR BOY
Michael Foreman

Barbed wire and barrage balloons, gas masks and Anderson shelters, loud bangs and piercing whines – the sights and sounds of war were all too familiar to a young boy growing up in the 1940s. Lowestoft, a quiet seaside town in Suffolk, was in the front line during World War II. Bombing raids, fires and trips to the air-raid shelters became almost daily events for young Michael Foreman and his friends.

EUROPE: UP AND AWAY
Sue Finnie

A lively book packed with information about Western Europe which includes sections on stamps, car numbers and languages as well as topics related to an individual country (from Flamenco dancing to frogs' legs).

Non-fiction from Dick King-Smith

COUNTRY WATCH

Animal watching can be fascinating and fun – if you know what to look out for and how best to observe it. There are so many different kinds of animals to see in the British countryside and it's not only the unusual ones that are interesting. *Country Watch* is full of surprising facts (did you know that the tiny mole can burrow its way through thirty pounds of earth in an hour?) and Dick King-Smith has lots of marvellous stories to tell about his own encounters with animals over the years.

TOWN WATCH

It's surprising how many wild animals there are to be seen in towns today. *Town Watch* is crammed with information about the many mammals, birds, insects and reptiles that live within the bounds of our towns and cities. Did you know that the cheeky house-sparrow is really one of the tough guys of the bird world, roaming the city in gangster-style mobs? From rubbish-tip pests like rats and cockroaches to protected species such as owls and bats, this book has a wealth of information and stories about urban wildlife.

WATER WATCH

If you look at a map of the world, you'll see that most of its surface is sea. We are surrounded by water – all around us there are lakes, ponds, rivers and streams – not to mention man-made waterways like canals. On holiday at the seaside you can enjoy identifying all the different kinds of gull, or if you're near a rocky coastline you might even see a seal! And there are all sorts of water birds – some with very unusual habits – living near lakes and marshes. You'd have to be lucky to spot an otter but if you're patient and observant, there are some fascinating animals to be spotted in and around a garden or village pond.

THE PUFFIN BOOK OF HANDWRITING
Tom Gourdie

How to write well with everyday materials. Write an alphabet in a tree of hearts, fill in word puzzles, trace letters, draw line patterns, have fun and acquire an elegant style of handwriting. These exercises have been devised to help you learn how to write beautifully.

THE PUFFIN BOOK OF DANCE
Craig Dodd

From ballet to Broadway, this book is packed with fascinating information for all young dance fans. From the evolution of dance in all its forms to dance classes, schools and techniques, the life of professional dancers, how dances are made and much more besides, this book captures the glamour and excitement of this spectacular art form.

WINGS AND THINGS
How an aircraft flies

Neil Ardley

How is it possible to get things with wings off the ground, and how ever do they stay in the air for long periods of time? Find out for yourself with this original and fascinating book. In addition to clear explanations, the author describes simple activities which vividly explain the principles of flight.

SNAP HAPPY
How a camera works

Neil Ardley

Lenses, films, shutters, flash – what are they and how do they enable a camera to take photos? In this informative book, the author describes in simple terms the basic principles of photography.

PETS FOR KEEP
Dick King-Smith

A light, amusing book of twelve simple pets, from hamsters to budgies, each with an anecdote and lots of useful and practical hints for pet owners and potential owners. No nonsense, just matter of fact and fun to read.

CHECK OUT CHESS
Bob Wade and Ted Nottingham

A basic guide for those learning to play chess. The moves each piece can make are described and there are a variety of exercises to familiarise the reader with them. The principles of checking, castling and so on are clearly explained, as are attacking, defending and the rudiments of tactics.